The most excellent book
of how to be a . .
magician

8-99

# The *most* *excellent* book of
# how to be a
# magician

*Peter Eldin*

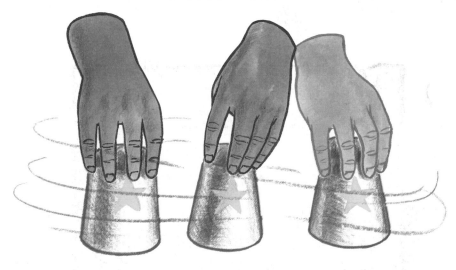

Copper Beech Books
Brookfield, Connecticut

© Aladdin Books Ltd 1996
*Designed and produced by*
Aladdin Books Ltd
28 Percy Street
London WIP 0LD

*First published in the United States in 1996 by*
Copper Beech Books,
an imprint of
The Millbrook Press
2 Old New Milford Road
Brookfield, Connecticut 06804

*Editor* Katie Roden
*Design* David West Children's Book Design
*Designer* Edward Simkins
*Illustrator* Rob Shone

Printed in Belgium

Library of Congress Cataloging-in-Publication Data
Eldin, Peter.The most excellent book of how to be a magician.
Peter Eldin: illustrated by Rob Shone.p. cm.Includes index.Summary: Provides instructions for a variety of tricks, from walking through a brick wall to linking paper clips in space, and advice on making the necessary costume and props and presenting your act to an audience.
ISBN 0-7613-0458-4 (lib. bdg.).
ISBN 0-7613-0473-8 (pbk.)
1. Conjuring--Juvenile literature.
2. Tricks--Juvenile literature. 3. Magicians--Juvenile literature.
[1. Magic tricks.] I. Shone, Rob, ill. II. Title.
GV1548.E364 1996
793.8--dc20 95-47143
CIP AC

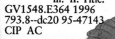

# CONTENTS

INTRODUCTION 3

LOOKING THE PART 4

PUTTING AN ACT TOGETHER 6

LINK-UP IN SPACE 8

A LONG STRETCH 9

THE DISAPPEARING COIN 10

THE MAGIC GLASS 11

STRING AND STRAW 12

TURNOVER TRICKERY 13

PURSE OF MYSTERY 14

RIP IT GOOD! 16

X-RAY MAGIC 18

MAGIC BALLS 20

TREASURE HUNT 22

RING ESCAPE 24

WATER TRAVEL 26

INVISIBLE WRITING 28

TUBE OF MYSTERY 30

INDEX AND GLOSSARY 32

# INTRODUCTION

There are many ways to entertain an audience but magic, or conjuring, is the most fascinating. It's not difficult to learn conjuring, and magic can be performed anywhere – in a theater, a living room, a classroom, or even on a bus – but the most important part of magic is to practice the tricks you learn.

As you read the book, look for these symbols:

★ shows the secret preparation you need to make before you perform your tricks.

✔ will give you tips on how to perfect your magic craft.

Everybody likes to see a magician

perform mind-boggling tricks. Now you can be that magician!

# *Looking the* PART

Wear a costume to make your act even more spectacular!

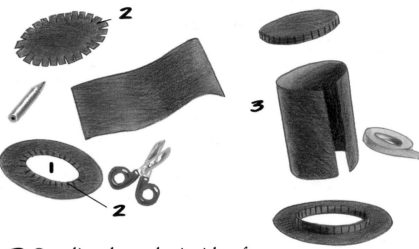

### The Top Hat

*You will need: 2 large circles of black cardboard; a wide rectangle of black cardboard; scissors; sticky tape; stars and glitter to decorate.*

❚ Cut a hole in one circle. Make sure it is big enough to fit onto your head.

**2** Cut slits along the inside of the hole, and along the outside of the full circle.

**3** Roll oblong cardboard into a tube, and tape the edges.

**4** Tape the circles to the inside of the tube. You can decorate your hat with glitter or bright paints.

✔ *Make a special table for your magic show. Glue together strong cardboard boxes, and decorate them with bright colors, magical symbols, or a cloth.*

# AN EXCELLENT MAGICIAN'S OUTFIT

**Magic wand**
Make your wand from a wooden dowel. Paint the ends white and the center black to make a traditional wand. If you want to be even more spectacular, use bright colors or glitter.

**Hat**
Once you have made a basic hat, you can use a similar pattern to invent all sorts of crazy designs.

**Bow tie**
Many joke shops sell bright bow ties, or you could make your own from brightly colored ribbon, felt, or crêpe paper, tied in a big bow, and pinned to your shirt.

**Vest**
A traditional piece of the magician's kit! See if you can borrow an old vest and decorate it with stars and magical symbols.

**Shirt**
Whatever shirt or top you choose, you need one with long sleeves to hide your secrets. But magicians do not use their sleeves as much as many people believe – they mainly rely on skill to create their illusions.

**Shoes and Pants**
Black is the traditional color worn by magicians, but if you don't have black pants, don't worry – make up your own crazy color scheme, and decorate your table to match!

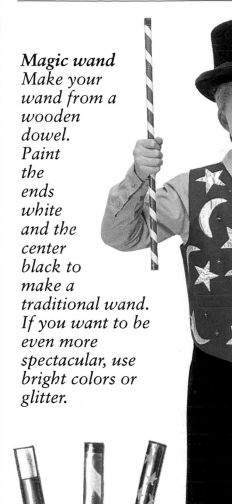

# *Putting an* ACT TOGETHER

## A few important rules of magic.

### Don't be a Bore!

Make sure your *patter* (conversation) is interesting, and your show is put together carefully before you perform it. Because you know how the tricks are done, you may feel like showing off. Don't. No one likes a braggart!

### Keep the Ideas Flowing!

Develop the tricks that you perform. Think hard about each trick and you may find ways of changing it to make it more spectacular or more entertaining for the audience.

### Practice Makes Perfect

The more you practice, the better you will be. And, you won't be quite so nervous when the time comes to perform!

### Keep it a Secret!

The secrets of magic are simple, but they need practice! If you do something clever, people will ask how it's done. If you tell them, all your work will be wasted. Never repeat a trick: The audience will watch you more closely the second time.

## My Magic Act

### Tricks

Props

1. Introduce myself

2. Purse of mystery...........Purse on table and wand up sleeve

3. Link-up in space...........Paper clips and paper on table

4. A long stretch...........Hanky on table

5. String and straw...........String, scissors, and prepared straw on table

6. Treasure hunt...........3 boxes on table, one marked with coin. 1 box and coin up right sleeve

7. X-ray magic...........Prepared cards, blindfold, and pen on table

8. Keep water travel ready, in case the audience wants another trick!

REMEMBER: DON'T MOVE RIGHT ARM TOO MUCH - THE COIN WILL RATTLE!

## Planning your Act

Start with a simple trick to grab people's attention. In the middle of the act use longer tricks, and end with a spectacular one.

Make a list of your act and of everything you need, and cross each item off the list as you put it on your table.

## What do I Say?

What you say (your patter) is important. If you talk during your act, you must practice your patter. It is a good idea to write it out and learn it by heart.

# *Link-up in* SPACE

## Two paper clips link themselves together...by magic!

**1** Take a piece of paper, 4 in. x 6 in. Hold it between your hands.

**2** Fold the right end of the paper toward your audience and then to the left.

**3** Place a paper clip over the two layers of paper.

**4** Fold the left end toward you, then to the right. Put a second paper clip over the two top layers of paper.

**5** Take one end of the paper in your left hand and the other end in your right.

**6** Tell the audience that the paper clips are far apart. Pull the paper in opposite directions. The paper clips will jump off the paper and link together!

*Clips are linked*

✔ *This trick works automatically, but you must pretend that it is very complicated and skillful. Practice until you can do it quickly.*

# A *Long* STRETCH

## The ever-growing handkerchief!

**1** Hold a large handkerchief by two corners and twist it between your hands. Secretly bunch some of the material into your hands.

**2** Pull the handkerchief tight, then pretend to stretch it. Twirl and stretch it again and again.

**3** Every so often, allow a bit of material to slip out. The twirling and stretching action makes it look as if the hanky is getting longer.

**4** Keep twirling and tightening until all the material has been released from your hands and you are holding only the corners of the handkerchief.

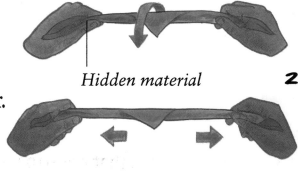

*Hidden material*

**5** Put both hands together. The hanky seems to have returned to its normal size.

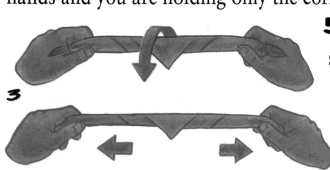

✔ *Try to convince the audience that you really are doing magic. The faster you perform, the more impressive it will be.*

# *The Disappearing* COIN

## Make a coin vanish magically!

**1** Show a coin to your audience, then place it in the center of a large piece of paper.

**2** Fold the paper once to the left, over the coin.

**3** Fold the paper again, from the top to the bottom so that the coin is tucked in the corner.

**4** Fold the paper again, from left to right.

**5** Hold the paper up, with the open end pointing downward, and say some magic words. Secretly shake the paper gently. Let the coin slip out of the paper and into your hand or your sleeve.

**6** Open the paper with a flourish, and show the audience that it is empty!

2

3

4

✔ *This trick works best if you perform it smoothly, without pausing between folds. Practice it until you can drop the coin accurately every time.*

# *The Magic* GLASS

## A simple but amazing illusion!

★ *You will need: 2 pieces of paper, both the same color; a glass; a coin; sticky tape; scissors; a handkerchief.*
*1. Cut out a circle of paper and stick it to the bottom of the glass with a small amount of tape.*
*2. Put the coin in the center of the paper and the glass on the edge before your show starts.*

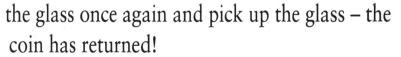

❶ Place the handkerchief over the glass.

❷ Lift up the glass and place it over the coin.

❸ Lift the handkerchief with a flourish – it will look as if the coin has disappeared!

❹ Place the handkerchief over the glass once again and pick up the glass – the coin has returned!

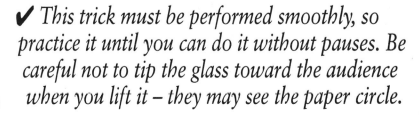

2

✔ *This trick must be performed smoothly, so practice it until you can do it without pauses. Be careful not to tip the glass toward the audience when you lift it – they may see the paper circle.*

# *String and* STRAW

## A string is cut in two...but stays unharmed!

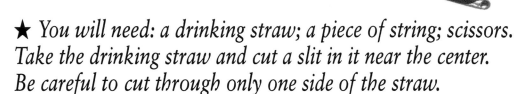

*Slit*

★ *You will need: a drinking straw; a piece of string; scissors. Take the drinking straw and cut a slit in it near the center. Be careful to cut through only one side of the straw.*

**1** Thread the string through the straw and bend it in half with the slit facing downward.

**2** Secretly pull on both ends of the string and it will poke through the slit.

**3** Cut the straw in half.

**4** Pull the string from the halves of the straw – it has magically "joined again" into one piece!

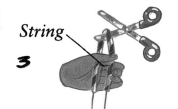

*String*

**2**

**3**

✔ *Carefully hide the string that has gone through the slit.*

# *Turnover* TRICKERY

## Two pieces of paper change places by magic!

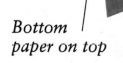

**1** Show two differently colored pieces of paper to your audience.

**2** Place one piece flat on your table and place the other on top of it.

**3** Roll up the pieces. Start rolling from the end nearest to you, and roll away from you.

**4** When you reach the end of the roll, allow the edge of the bottom piece to make one more half-turn onto the table.

**5** Unroll the paper toward you. The two pieces have magically swapped places!

**3**

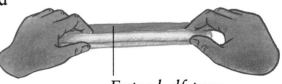

*Extra half-turn* **4**

*Bottom paper on top*

✔ *This trick is very simple, but it needs practice. Keep trying it until you find the point at which the bottom piece flips over and until you know when to unroll the pieces to make the trick work perfectly.*

# Purse of MYSTERY

## Pull a long magic wand from a tiny purse!

★ *You will need: a small purse (borrow an old one, or buy a cheap one from a secondhand store); scissors; your magic wand; ribbon.*

*Cut hole*

1. Cut a hole in the bottom of the purse, big enough to push the wand through.

2. Push the wand up your left sleeve and tie it to your arm with the ribbon.

**2**

❙ Show the audience that the purse is empty.

**2** Put the purse in your left hand, over the wand. Make sure the audience can't see the hole.

**3** Open the purse with your right fingers.

**4** Pretend that you are looking for some money. Reach into the purse, grab the wand through the hole and slowly pull it from your sleeve and out of the purse.

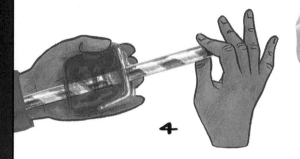

**4**

✔ *It is important to attach the wand on the side of your arm facing away from the audience, so they cannot see that it is coming from your sleeve. To convince the audience that the purse really is magic, pull the wand slowly from the purse and show great surprise as you do. You can adapt this trick in many ways – for example, try it with a long string of colored handkerchiefs instead of the wand.*

# *Rip It* GOOD!

## Rip up a strip of paper...then fix it again!

★ *You will need: 2 strips of paper, about 2 in. x 6 in.; glue.*
*1. Fold one of the strips into a neat little package and glue this onto the end of the other strip.*

*2. Keep this prepared strip in your pocket during your act. When it is time to perform the trick, take it in your hands.*

Glue

❙ Stretch the paper between your hands and show it to the audience. Keep the little package hidden safely in your hand, so that the audience thinks the paper is ordinary.

**2**

Hidden package

**2** Rip the strip in half and put the left half in front of the right half. Rip the strip again and again. Keep ripping until all the pieces of paper are about the same size as the folded strip.

**3** Close your hand around the pieces of paper and blow on them. At the same time, turn the paper over in your hands so that the folded strip is toward the front, closest to the audience.

**4** Pull open the folded strip, keeping the ripped pieces hidden in your hand.

*Keep torn paper hidden*

**5** Everyone will applaud this great feat of magic. As they do, casually crumple up the strip and the hidden pieces in your hands, and put them into your pocket.

✔ *Practice until you can hide the folded paper perfectly in your hand, and act as if the paper is ordinary.*

# X-ray MAGIC

## Reveal your amazing powers of prediction!

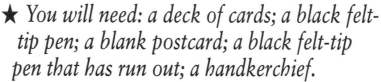

★ *You will need: a deck of cards; a black felt-tip pen; a blank postcard; a black felt-tip pen that has run out; a handkerchief.*

*1. Mark the Seven of Hearts with an "X" and return it to the deck.*

*2. Using the working pen, write on the postcard: "You will choose the Seven of Hearts." Put it upside down on your table. You do not need the working pen for this trick.*

**2**

**Cards must face volunteer**

❚ Blindfold a volunteer with the handkerchief.

**2** Pick up the postcard so the writing faces you. Pretend to write on it, with the empty pen, then put it face down on your table. Don't let anyone see what's on it!

**3** Give the volunteer the cards and empty pen. Ask him or her to mark an "X" on any card, then shuffle the cards. Don't let anyone see that the pen is empty.

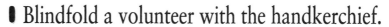

**4** Remove the blindfold. Ask the volunteer to read the card.

**5** Ask another volunteer to find the marked card.
It's the Seven of Hearts!

✔ *Pretend to read the volunteer's mind before writing on the postcard.*

# *Magic* BALLS

## A simple trick that never fails to impress!

★ *You will need: 3 plastic cups (decorate them with bright colors); 2 balls of crumpled tinfoil – make sure that the cups will fit over them.*

*1. Place the cups on your table, with one ball under a cup. Faintly mark this cup with a pencil.*

*2. Leave the second ball on the table.*

❚ Place the second ball under a cup.

**2** Swap the cups around quickly, telling the audience to keep their eyes on the cup containing the ball. Hold the cups firmly, so that you can feel the balls inside and know where they are.

**3** Stop swapping. Ask an audience member to point to the cup containing the ball.

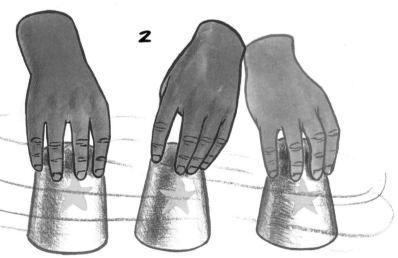

**4** Pick up the cup. If it contains a ball, squeeze its sides so you lift the ball up too. The cup will appear empty!

**5** Lift the marked cup, but leave the ball on the table.

The audience will be amazed! You can repeat this trick many times – it never fails to astound your audience!

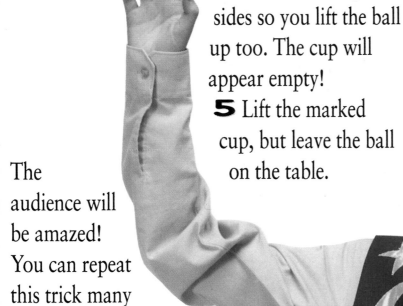

✔ *Don't tilt the cups toward the audience when you lift them: They will be able to see the balls.*

4

# *Treasure* HUNT

## Can the audience find the magic box?

★ *You will need: 4 identical small boxes; a piece of ribbon; 2 small coins; clay.*

*1. Put one coin in a box.*

*2. Use the ribbon to tie that box to your right wrist so that it is hidden by your sleeve.*

Coin hidden in box

*3. Push a small piece of clay into one of the three remaining boxes. Make a small pencil mark on this box so you know which one it is.*

*4. Place the three boxes and the coin on your table.*

❙ Show the three boxes and the coin to your audience.

**2** With your left hand, put the coin into the marked box. Secretly push the coin into the clay, so that it can't move.

**3** Close the box and shake it in your right hand. The audience will think they can hear the coin rattling in the box. The noise really comes from the hidden box.

**4** Mix the three boxes on the table and ask someone to point to the one containing the coin. Shake the chosen box with your left hand. As no noise is heard, everyone will think that the box is empty.

*Hidden coin makes noise*

**5** Keep mixing the boxes and asking people to pick one. Every box will seem empty if you shake it with your left hand.

**6** At the end of the trick, use your right hand to pick up the marked box with the coin. Shake it in your right hand, and the hidden coin will be heard rattling.

**7** Open the box and take out the coin.

✔ *It is important to practice this trick, so that you know which arm to use when. As you take the coin out at the end, secretly wipe any clay off it.*

# *Ring* ESCAPE

## Use your magic powers to release a ring!

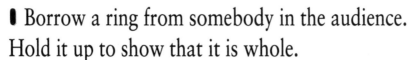

**1** Borrow a ring from somebody in the audience. Hold it up to show that it is whole.

**2** Fold some string in half and thread it through the ring.

**3** Take the ends of the string and push them through the center loop. Pull the knot tight.

**4** Ask for two volunteers from the audience and ask them to stand on either side of you.

**5** Hand one end of the string to the person on your right and the other end to the person on your left.

**6** Show the audience that the ring is knotted onto the middle of the rope. Tell them that it is impossible for the ring to escape from the string.

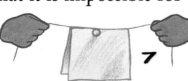

**7** Drape a handkerchief over the ring.

**8** Place your hands under the handkerchief and pull the loop down so that it goes around the bottom part of the ring. The ring is now free from the string.

**9** Pull the handkerchief away with a flourish and show the ring to the audience.

**8**

It looks as if the ring has passed right through the string!

✔ *Practice this trick so that you can tie the ring on quickly and without looking. The audience should not be able to see exactly what you do. They must not realize that it is a trick knot. Keep a curtain ring handy, in case you can't find a ring to borrow.*

# *Water* TRAVEL

## A cup of water moves through space!

★ *You will need: 2 paper bags; 2 paper cups; a jug of water; scissors.*
*1. Cut the bottom out of one of the cups, and place it inside the other cup. Together, they should look just like one ordinary cup.*
*2. Place the specially prepared cups (put together), the two bags, and the jug of water on your table.*

❚ Pick up the cup (although there are two cups you must pretend that there is only one) and pour some water into it.

**2** Tell your audience that you will make the water travel from one bag to the other. As you do, put the prepared cup into the first bag, then pretend to take it out again right away, as if you are demonstrating what you are going to do. In fact, you should leave the bottom cup in the first bag and take out only the inner cup, which will contain no water.

**3** Place this cup in the second bag.

**4** Pick up the second bag and then crush it between your hands (with the cup inside).

**5** Return to the first bag, lift out the cup, and pour the water back into the jug.

✔ *To perform this trick successfully, you must handle the two cups as if they are just one. Don't hesitate between putting the cup into the first bag and taking out the inner cup. Remember to hold the inner cup close to your table, so that the audience cannot see that it is bottomless. Pretend that the cup is heavy with water and you must handle it carefully.*

# *Invisible* WRITING

## A pen vanishes – under the audience's noses!

★ *You will need: a ball point pen with a small hole in its cap; a piece of thin elastic which is slightly shorter than your sleeve; a safety pin; a piece of paper; a large, colorful handkerchief.*

1. *Take the cap off the pen and thread the elastic through the hole.*

2. *Tie a knot in one end of the elastic. Pull the elastic tight so that the knot is hidden inside the cap.*

3. *Using the safety pin, carefully attach the other end of the elastic to the inside of your left sleeve, near the shoulder.*

4. *Push the pen back into the cap so it hangs just inside your sleeve. Put your right hand up your left sleeve, grab the pen and pull it down until your fingers can hold the cap.*

*Safety pin*

❙ Pull the pen from the cap and ask a member of your audience to write on the paper with it, to prove that it is real.

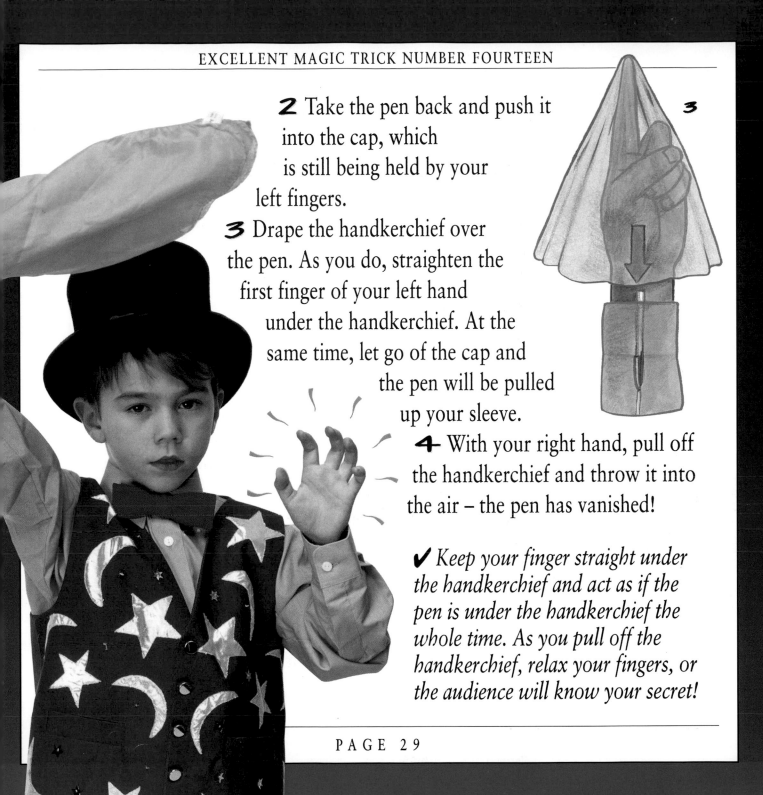

**2** Take the pen back and push it into the cap, which is still being held by your left fingers.

**3** Drape the handkerchief over the pen. As you do, straighten the first finger of your left hand under the handkerchief. At the same time, let go of the cap and the pen will be pulled up your sleeve.

**4** With your right hand, pull off the handkerchief and throw it into the air – the pen has vanished!

✔ *Keep your finger straight under the handkerchief and act as if the pen is under the handkerchief the whole time. As you pull off the handkerchief, relax your fingers, or the audience will know your secret!*

# Tube of MYSTERY

## A spectacular way to end your show!

★ *You will need: lots of brightly colored handkerchiefs; a larger handkerchief; dark thread; a sheet of thin cardboard; sticky tape.*

*1. Wrap the colored handkerchiefs in the large handkerchief.*

*2. Tie the corners of the big handkerchief together with the thread and make a large loop in the thread.*

*3. Put this bundle (magicians call this a "load") up your left sleeve, with the loop hanging out.*

*4. Roll the cardboard into a tube which is big enough to fit over your arm, and use a piece of tape to hold it together.*

Hidden load

❚ Place the tube over your left hand and slide it up onto your arm. This will prove to the audience that it is completely empty, so will make your trick even more impressive.

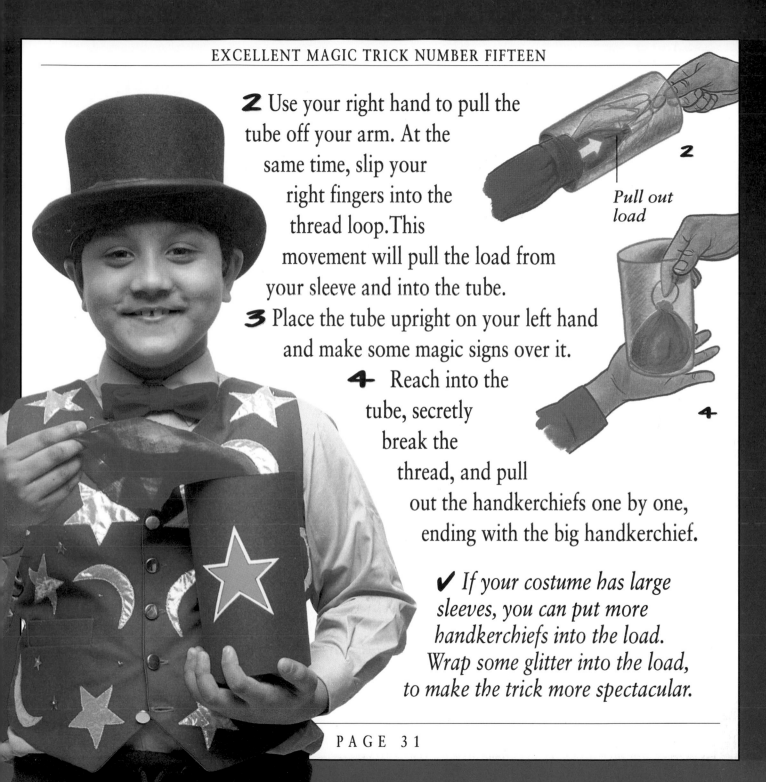

**2** Use your right hand to pull the tube off your arm. At the same time, slip your right fingers into the thread loop. This movement will pull the load from your sleeve and into the tube.

**3** Place the tube upright on your left hand and make some magic signs over it.

**4** Reach into the tube, secretly break the thread, and pull out the handkerchiefs one by one, ending with the big handkerchief.

**2**

*Pull out load*

**4**

✔ *If your costume has large sleeves, you can put more handkerchiefs into the load. Wrap some glitter into the load, to make the trick more spectacular.*

# *Magic* WORDS

**Audience** All the people who come to watch your show.

**Butterflies** The uncomfortable feeling that some people get in their stomachs when they are nervous.

**Conjuring** Another word for performing magic.

**Illusion** Convincing the audience that what you show them is real.

**Load** The magician's word for a hidden object which will be used in a trick.

**Patter** The jokes and conversation you use during your act.

**Props** All the objects that you use during your act.

# *Even More* MAGIC

If you want to learn more about magic, there are lots of magic books in shops or libraries. Try to join a local magic club – or form one of your own!

# INDEX

acting  8, 9, 17, 19, 27, 29

card tricks  18–19

coin tricks  10, 11, 22–23

costume  4–5

developing act  6–7, 15, 31

illusions  9, 12, 14–16, 20–21, 24–25, 26–27, 28–29

paper tricks  8, 13, 16–17

patter  6, 7

props  4

**Picture credits**
All pictures by Roger Vlitos